Astrid Berger • Gabriele Broniowski

Aufsteigen ... Englisch 3 Schularbeiten

So schaffst du die 3. Klasse HS/AHS und Neue Mittelschule

G&G

TEST 1

I FOCUS ON GRAMMAR:

1 Fill in the correct tense (present perfect or past tense):

1. Some years ago Liam ___________ (fly) to Valemount, Canada, to visit his father. One day he _______________ (go) fishing with his friend Ulva. When they saw some dark clouds, they ________________ (try) to build a shelter. On the way back Liam __________ (hurt) his leg but a search party __________________ (find) them.
2. ________________________ (you, ever, have) such an exciting adventure? - No, but I think a trip to Canada would be fun.
3. "Would you like to go cycling with me?" Sam asked. "Sorry, I can't" Tom answered. " I _________________________ (not, finish) studying for the test."
4. Do you know Mike, our neighbour's son? -Yes, I do. -Well, he ________________ (dye) his hair green yesterday.-That's cool. I _________________________ (never, dye) my hair before because my mother thinks I'll look awful.

2. Camping in Yosemite Park - Fill in the missing words.

finally – suddenly – first – last year – after several minutes – then – from time

_______________ my parents and I stayed at a little campsite in Yosemite Park. _______________ we put up our tent and ________________ we wanted to roast some marshmallows. My dad told me to get some firewood, so we could make a fire.

______________________ we were sitting in front of our tent enjoying our marshmallows.

____________________ to time we heard strange noises. I was afraid but my dad said that these noises were nothing unusual in the wilderness. _________________ we saw two racoons coming towards us. We quickly ran to our car and got inside.

The racoons ate all our food. ______________________________ the racoons left again.

3. Write down how long it took people to do things:

1. Mrs Kerny - three hours - do the ironing
2. she - twenty minutes - load the dishwasher
3. the rescue team - two days - find the survivors of the plane crash.

4. Fill in past tense simple or progressive:

1. When I phoned my friends they __________________________ (play) a new computer game.
2. When Bob _________________________ (do) the washing up he cut his finger.
3. I __________________________ (walk) to school when a dog ____________________ (attack) me.
4. My sister _________________________ (watch) her favourite TV series when the telephone ______________________ (ring).
5. Yesterday at seven I __________________________ (prepare) dinner for my family.

II READING COMPREHENSION

Read the text, then mark the statements true or false

Stuck in the Desert

Three years ago in January, Karim had a big problem. He will never forget that day.

The story began when his uncle, his brother, and Karim went to the desert. His uncle was the oldest, he was 70 years old, but he was still strong. His brother was 12 and Karim was 23 years old. All of them liked hunting. Usually they went hunting at the weekend, especially in winter, because winter is the hunting season in Saudi Arabia.

On the 27th of January, they decided to go hunting. They packed everything into their four-wheel-drive Range Rover and took off. It took them three hours by car to reach the place they were looking for. First, they put up the tent, then they made coffee and had a few minutes of rest. After that, they left to go hunting. They hunted using a falcon (=Falke). They spent two hours without finding anything. They decided to go back to the camp. On their way back, Karim's brother saw a rabbit. He cried, "Rabbit!! Rabbit! Quick!" Karim took the falcon's head cover off. When the rabbit saw the falcon, it ran fast, but Karim's falcon was a professional hunter. After two minutes, the rabbit was caught. They took it and went back to the camp where they started to cook their dinner. They ate the delicious food, drank some coffee, and sat around the fire talking until late in the evening. Then they went to bed.

They left camp the next day in the morning. They went north. Suddenly the car got stuck in the sand! They spent about three hours trying to pull out the car without success. Finally, they decided that Karim should try to get help. He took a bottle of water with him and started to walk south. He knew the way well, but it was a long way in the sand. Karim walked more than four hours without stopping. He felt tired and thirsty. Soon there was only little water left in his bottle. He stopped to rest for a while. When he got up again it was already dark. Suddenly, he met a man who was riding a camel. Karim asked him to take him to the road and he did. After that, Karim found a car, which took him to the city to get help. It took Karim one day to get back to his uncle and brother.

	True	False
Winter is the hunting season, so they went hunting in January.		
The Range Rover had four-wheel-drive.		
During the first two hours they found animals to hunt.		
The falcon could not catch the rabbit.		
The group sat around the fire until late in the evening.		
They could not go on because they ran out of petrol.		
Karim walked for more than four hours.		
Karim did not know the way and got lost.		
Karim met a man on a camel.		
The man took Karim to a road.		

III WRITING TASK

Look at the pictures, then write a text of about 120-150 words.

TEST 2

I FOCUS ON GRAMMAR

1. Complete the following if-clauses:

1. If you train your dog, it ______________________________ (guard your house).
2. He will buy a guinea pig for his children if they ________________ (promise) to take care of it.
3. If she goes on holiday, her brother ___________________________ (usually look after) her pets.
4. I will take riding lessons if I _________________________________ (not be allergic to) horses.

2. Comparisons: as.......as // ....than. Write 2 sentences each! Use the adjectives given.

1. Tom 1,75 m	Peter 1,85 m	John 1,75 m	tall/short
2. cinema 200 people	theatre 500 people	concert 1000 people	many/few
3. jeans £ 50	shoes £ 50	T-shirt £ 10	expensive/cheap

3. Fill in the correct forms of the past tense simple or progressive:

1. They ________________________ (play) Monopoly when they ____________________ (hear) a terrible cry.
2. I _______________________________ (do) my homework when the computer ________________________ (break down).
3. The girl in the thriller ______________________________ (wait) for her father when she ___________________________________ (see) a strange man with a woman and a little boy.
4. When the Inspector _______________________________ (knock) at the door the suspects (=Verdächtigen) ___________________________________ (watch) TV.

4. Fill in the correct tenses:

1. We __________________________ (not see) Charles since May. I don't know what he is doing.
2. The rain has stopped. The sun ________________________ (shine) now. Let's go out!
3. She ___________________________ (pick up) her aunt at the station tomorrow.
4 ______________________________ (you/ever/read) any of the "Harry Potter" books?
5. Yesterday Kate and Susan ______________________________ (show) me the photos they ___________________________ (take) in London in summer.
6. You _______________________________ (nicht müssen) do the homework today.

II WRITING TASK

Look at the pictures and write a story of about 120-150 words

TEST 3

I FOCUS ON GRAMMAR

1. Adjective or adverb?

1. They chatted ________________ (happy) all afternoon because they had not seen each other since the holidays.
2. Susan is a very ________________ (good) student. She always does her homework ________________ (careful).
3. My brother always looks ________________ (angry) after talking to my dad. He thinks our dad is too strict.
4. Jennifer felt ________________ (terrible) cold when she came home from a walk with the dog.
5. Paul didn't want to miss the bus, so he ran very ________________ (fast) to catch it.
6. They got stuck in a traffic jam so they ________________ (near) missed the plane.
7. Are you sure you want to eat this soup? It tastes ________________ (awful).

2. Use the correct tenses (present simple/progressive, past simple/progressive, present perfect, future):

1. ________________ (you ever try) bungee jumping? – Yes, I ________________ (do) that last year, but I think it's too dangerous.
2. I hope Aunt Jane ________________ (come) to visit us next week. I haven't seen her for weeks.
3. In 2002 Fred ________________ (not understand) a word of English, but now he ________________ (speak) it quite well.
4. Right now my mother ________________ (buy) food at the supermarket. She ________________ (go) there every Thursday.
5. Do you know what ________________ (happen) yesterday? I ________________ (watch) my favourite TV show when we suddenly ________________ (have) a power failure (=Stromausfall).

3. Complete the following if-clauses:

1. Maria will get you some money if she ________________ (go) to the bank.
2. You have a bad cold. If you go to the doctor he ________________ (tell) you what to do.
3. If he hits his little brother, his father always ________________ (punish=bestrafen) him.
4. If my alarm clock does not go off I ________________ (be always) late for school.
5. I'll give her a call if I ________________ (find) her phone number. I don't know where I put it.

II READING COMPREHENSION

Read the text, then complete the sentences below:

A Day in the Life of a Pet Dog

My name is Kim and I am a dog. Many humans do not understand me, but my life is really quite simple: I like to play, play, play. The best time to play is in the morning. I go out into the garden and start gnawing (=herumnagen) on one of the pieces of wood I keep lying around in the garden. Sometimes I try to get my human to throw me a little tennis ball.

I also love soft toys. My favourite part is the inside. It's like a challenge (=Herausforderung) to see how fast I can get to the <u>stuffing</u>. I've found that using my teeth and claws together works best.

My next favourite game is when my human takes me for a walk. I let her put a leash on me because she likes to think that she's the boss. We both know the truth, though, namely that I rule the house.

I like being in the woods. It's fun to run around without a leash, to sniff at all the trees, and to jump into the nearby river. I love swimming.

Sometimes we meet my friend Woody. Then we chase (=jagen) each other. That's a lot of fun.

The only times I like to take a break from playing are for eating and sleeping. Sometimes I only pretend (=vortäuschen) that I am asleep, so my human does not pay any attention to me. I'm lucky because my basket is in the living room. All I need is for the phone to ring and then I can jump onto the sofa. It is wonderful to have that big sofa all to myself.

I never waste any food. If my human leaves any food on the table, I eat it, of course! I love cheese and bananas best!

At night, my human is a really good actor. She tells me to sleep under the bed but just when she's almost asleep, she loves it when I lick her face or jump onto the bed.

It's one of the highlights of her day!

Complete the following sentences:

In the morning Kim runs out into the garden......

To get to the inside of the soft toy Kim....

Her human thinks that.....

In the woods Kim thinks it is fun ....

Kim loves playing but she also likes.....

III WRITING TASK:

In August you spent three days on a lake in the Sierra Nevada with a friend. On the last day there was a terrible snowstorm, but you survived. Now, six weeks later, you write a letter to a friend in which you tell him/her about your adventure. (± 120-150 words)

Look at the following words. Use as many as possible for your letter:

fishing – tent – campfire – snowstorm – shelter (Schutzbehausung) – cold – hurt – search party – hunters – helicopter – hospital – stay in bed

TEST 4

I FOCUS ON GRAMMAR

1. Put the verb into the past simple or the past progressive:

1 Last night I ________________ (read) in bed when I suddenly ________________ (hear) a scream.

2. ________________ (you, watch) television last night when I ________________ (phone) you?

3. I ________________ (break) a plate last night. I ________________ (do) the washing up when it ________________ (slip = rutschen) out of my hand.

4. Someone ________________ (run) off with my clothes while I ________________ (swim).

5. The thieves ________________ (break) in while we ________________ (sleep).

2. Fill in the correct tenses:

1. We ________________ (not be) to the cinema since June.
2. It is ________________ (rain) now. Let's not go out!
3. We ________________ (can meet) him at the airport tomorrow .
4. ________________ (you/ever/watch) "Spongebob"?
5. Yesterday Tina ________________ (to show) me the video she ________________ (make) at Christmas.
6. Last year I ________________ (walk) to the office every day.

3. Find the correct modal verbs:

1. We have lots of time we ________________ (nicht müssen) hurry.
2. Last year he ________________ (müssen) give up smoking.
3. They think he ________________ (können) to leave the hospital in 4 days.
4. Sorry, I didn't come yesterday but I ________________ (nicht dürfen) to leave my room.
5. I ________________ orget to phone George (nicht dürfen).
6. Why ________________ (you/müssen) leave so early yesterday?
7. This is a wonderful book! You ________________ (müssen) read it!
8. I didn't like the soup at all. I was very happy I ________________ (nicht müssen) eat it.
9. I'm very busy tomorrow. So I ________________ (nicht können) see you.
10. ________________ (können) you open the window, please? It's hot in here!
11. Oh, you ________________ (nicht müssen) help me. I can do it myself.
12. Be careful! We ________________ (nicht dürfen) not break the window!

II READING COMPREHENSION

Read the following text and mark the sentences true or false

Ghosts of London

Are there such things as ghosts? Some people say no, others say yes. Nobody can really say for sure that ghosts exist, but at some places around London there seem to be ghosts, places such as Minster House. You can decide for yourself if you think that a ghost really lives there.
Minster House, built by John Harris, is on Plummer Street. It is a beautiful old house. The Harris family lived in the house for five generations, and people say that the daughter of John Harris still comes to the house as a ghost.
Grand balls and parties were very popular in the nineteenth century (Jahrhundert), and the Harris daughters were having a party one night. Sarah Harris was being courted (wurde verehrt) by a young military officer. The young officer's name was Wenman Wynniatt, and when Sarah asked him if he would be coming to her party, he answered, "Oh yes, I'll be there."
The night of the party Sarah waited and waited for Wynniatt and in the end she was sure that he was not going to come. Suddenly he appeared before her, but when she stretched out (ausstrecken) her hand to him, he just walked right past her, without seeming to recognize her. This was the last time she saw him, and his body was found the next morning on the banks (Ufer) of the Thames river. His watch had stopped at the exact moment he had appeared at the party. Although Sarah never saw him again, people have seen the ghost of a young man in Minster House very often, and they think that maybe the young man is still trying to keep his promise to Sarah.

1. We can be sure that ghosts exist.	true	☐	false	☐
2. John Plummer built Minster House.	true	☐	false	☐
3. Sarah's boy-friend was a young officer.	true	☐	false	☐
4. Wynniatt did not want to come to the party.	true	☐	false	☐
5. Sarah saw Wynniatt at the party.	true	☐	false	☐
6. Wynniatt's body was found in the river Thames.	true	☐	false	☐
7. The ghost of an old man appears in Minster House.	true	☐	false	☐

III WRITING TASK

Rules in the family

Choose one of the teenagers and <u>write a short text</u> (100 words) about the rules in their families. <u>Use 'must not' and ' need not'</u>.

TEST 5

I FOCUS ON GRAMMAR

1. Modal verbs

1. Imagine, Tim missed his flight, so he ____________________ (müssen) spend a night in an expensive hotel and ____________________ (können) only fly the next day.
2. ____________________________ (you/dürfen) go to the cinema yesterday?
3. Sorry, I ____________________________ (nicht können) go to the match with you next Monday.
4. You __________________________ (nicht müssen) wait for me.
5. Patrick told me that he _________________________ (nicht dürfen) go to the concert next week because of his bad marks.
6. We ___________________________ (müssen) walk to school if my mother doesn't take us there by car.
7. In the evening we __________________________ (nicht dürfen) be too loud because of our neighbour's baby.
8. Imagine, we __________________________ (nicht müssen) pay for the tickets last night, they gave them to us for free.

2. Fill in the correct prepositions:

Yesterday was a perfect day as there were no clouds _____ the sky.

Who is that old lady _____ the picture? She looks familiar.

Mrs. Anderson's office is _____ the second floor.

We always get a lot of homework _____ Friday.

Her father thinks that _____ 13 Mary is too young to go to the disco.

I left all my English books _____ school because we have no homework today.

She has been _____ the phone for hours! Who is she talking to?

Where is your dad? – He is _____ work.

Could you put he book _____ the table, please?

She wants to live _____ the country because the air is much cleaner there.

_____ July they always go on holiday with their parents.

3. Some, something, somebody, somewhere or any, anything, anybody, anywhere?

1. I'm sure ____________________ will be there to help you with the suitcase.
2. I can't see my mother ____________________. Do you know where she is?
3. We can't see ____________________. It's so dark in here.
4. ____________________ people are really terrible. They can't remember ____________________.

5. The new bookshop is no good. There are not ______________________ interesting books.
6. Agnes was so shocked that she didn't say ________________________ .

II READING COMPREHENSION

Animals in Danger

Whales have been hunted for food and other products for thousands of years. In the 19th century (Jahrhundert) man began to kill so many whales that they became an endangered (gefährdet) species. At that time man invented a better harpoon (Harpune), had faster boats and better machines to kill whales with. Even the giant blue whale, weighing up to 180 tons and 31 metres long, could be killed now.

Each blue whale produced about 30 tons of oil. So whale hunters wanted to kill these animals because they could earn a lot of money. 1930 was the worst year. In that year 30,000 of these wonderful animals were killed.

Today experts think that there are fewer than 1,000 blue whales left. Before hunters began to kill so many whales there had been a quarter of a million animals. Hunting is now officially banned (verboten). Only Japan and Norway still kill whales.

Dolphins, which have developed (entwickelt) a special "friendship" with humans, are also threatened (bedroht) by pollution and people. Thousands of dolphins are killed every year in tuna fishermen's nets. In parts of the Pacific Ocean the number of dolphins has fallen by more than 80% since 1959.

Choose the answer which tells what the text really says:

1. Whales have been hunted	for hundreds of years
	since the 19th century
	for thousands of years
2. The giant blue whale	is up to 31 metres long
	does no longer exist
	weighs up to 30 tonnes
3. Whales are still killed by	Greenpeace
	Norway and Japan
	fishermen's nets

Answer in complete sentences:

1. Why were more whales killed in the 19th century and later?
2. Why do people hunt whales?

III WRITING TASK

You are on holiday with your parents. You are spending one week in London. Write a short letter from London to your best friend back home telling him/her about your stay.

Test 6

I FOCUS ON GRAMMAR

1. Word Order

1. Tom/Last Saturday/his friends/met/at the cinema
2. such/eaten/I/never/good/have/pizza/a
3. that/Sarah/she/me/had/keys/found/told /her
4. at/They/often/after/park/meet/the/school
5. lunch/just/We/finished/have/our
6. evening/you/in/Will/the/home/be/at?

2. Fill in the Prepositions (in, at, to, by, after, on, behind)

______ Tuesday Bill met his friends ______ the evening. They went ______ the cinema. The film began ________ 9 o'clock pm. Bill was sitting _________ a very tall lady. _______ the film the friends went home _______ bus. _______ the next day Bill was very tired. ______ school he could not concentrate.

3. Past simple or progressive?

Yesterday I __________________________ (read) a book when the phone __________________________ (ring). It was my friend Sandra. She __________________________ (wait) for her train to arrive and __________________________ (want) to know if I __________________________ (have) time to meet her. She __________________________ (ask) me what I __________________________ (do) at the moment. I __________________________ (told) her I was free and that we could meet in 40 minutes. While I __________________________ (look) for my keys my dog Wayne __________________________ (bark) all the time because he wanted to come with me.

II READING COMPREHENSION

Molly and the vampire next door

Molly was an old lady. She had a son, Charles, who was married to Yvonne. And she had a very nice neighbour. Molly knew that he was a vampire. "Cornelius is a very nice vampire. He lives in a tiny (winzig) flat in the old house next to mine. He always asks me what he can do for me to make my life easier", Molly said. Charles and Yvonne only shook their heads. They did not believe in vampires. And they never saw this Cornelius when they came to visit Molly. "Of course, you don't see him! He is asleep during the day. As I told you, he is a vampire. Vampires are creatures of the night", Molly explained.

One day Charles came to see Molly and told her that it was no longer safe for her to live alone. She was too old and he was sure his mother would be much happier in a retirement home (Altersheim). Molly was shocked. She did not want to leave her nice little house in the country with the beautiful garden, and she did not want to leave Cornelius. He was much more than a friend. She could not imagine a life without him.

In the evening she went into the garden, sat down on a bench and cried because she was so unhappy. When it was dark Cornelius found her there. "What is the matter with you, Molly? Why are you crying?" So Molly told him everything. "How can Charles do this to me? I don't want to lose everything I love! Charles doesn't love me. I've done everything for him after his father died when Charles was only 10." Cornelius was very understanding (verständnisvoll) and tried to comfort (trösten) Molly. "You know what, Cornelius", Molly said suddenly.
"I want to stay with you. You are such a nice man, we love each other. I don't mind that you are a vampire." "Well, that's such a good idea", Cornelius said. "We could live in my cousin Archibald's castle in Scotland. You will like it there. And you will like Archibald's wife, Irene. She likes knitting and she mixes wonderful blood-orange cocktails."

So Molly and Cornelius moved to Scotland. When Charles came to take his mother to the retirement home he could not find her. He never saw Molly again. Cornelius and Molly lived happily in Scotland. And Molly learned how to make wonderful blood-orange cocktails.

Answer the following questions:

1. Why did Charles and Yvonne never see Cornelius?
2. Where did Cornelius live?
3. Why was Molly so sad?
4. When did Molly's husband die?
5. Who was Archibald?
6. Where did Archibald live?
7. Do you believe in vampires? Why/Why not?

III WRITING TASK

Look at the pictures and write a story of about 120-150 words.

Test 7

I FOCUS ON GRAMMAR

1. Fill in modal verbs:

Yesterday I ______________________ (nicht müssen) help my mother with the washing up.
It was my birthday and so my mother said I ______________________
(dürfen) read while my brother and my sister ______________________ (müssen) load the dishwasher and to clean the table.
In the evening I ______________________ (nicht können) find my English book,
so I ______________________ (müssen) call my friend who lives next door. She came and we did our homework together.
I am happy that I ______________________ (nicht müssen) tell my English teacher today that
I ______________________ (nicht können) do my homework yesterday.

2. Fill in the correct prepositions (to, on, before, for, at, in):

While Sue was ______________ holiday ______________ Florida she stayed ______________ her friend Barbara's house. ______________ one of Barbara's parties she met this cool guy, Frank.
______________ the next day he called her ______________ the morning.
"Do you want to meet me ______________ Friday ______________ seven o'clock?", he asked.
Sue was so happy.
When Sue was ______________ home again she told her friends about the great time she had had in Florida. ______________ she went back to school she wrote a letter ______________ Barbara to thank her ______________ the wonderful holiday.

3. Fill in the correct tenses:

1. Can you hear that noise? I think our neighbour ______________________ (play) the trumpet.
2. America ______________________ (discover) in 1492.
3. Tigers ______________________ (eat) meat.
4. Yesterday I ______________________ (see) my teacher at the cinema.
   When I ______________________ (come) in she ______________________ (talk) to a strange looking man.
5. Next year Paul ______________________ (spend) his holidays in Turkey.

II READING COMPREHENSION

The Ravens

George and Ann were two of the ravens that lived at the Tower of London, in England. Most of the time they enjoyed life there, but some days things got too much for them. Ann and George loved to sit on the wall and watch the people go by. Sometimes they laughed at some of the silly things they did. But they didn't like people to stop at the wall to stare at them, make faces at them, or take pictures of them.

"Not another group of photographers," George complained. "I think they have taken about five hundred pictures of me today."

In the evening George told the other ravens that he had had enough and wanted to leave.

Ann said, "George, we can't leave here. We can't even fly. They clipped (beschneiden) our wings so we can't leave. I heard a Beefeater guard say once that as long as there were ravens at the Tower of London, England would stay a mighty (mächtig) country. If we leave, then what will happen to England?"

But George did not care. He had a plan. On the next day he showed his friends a sign he had made.

"STUFFED (ausgestopft) RAVENS. ONE POUND EACH. DROP YOUR COIN INTO THE CUP AND CARRY ONE HOME! HAVE ONE OF YOUR VERY OWN!"

"Let's stand right here on the wall as usual. Put the sign next to us, Ann. Don't forget the cup and hurry up. Some people are coming."

So the ravens stood perfectly still. Two children came walking by and stopped to read the sign.

"Oh look, Jessica. For one pound we can have a stuffed raven. Do you have a pound coin? I want one," David asked. "No, David. I've only got 50p. "I guess we can't have a raven," David said, and then the three children walked away.

Next, a man and a woman came. They walked up to the ravens. "Look at the stuffed birds, Alex. I want one. They're so cute," the woman giggled (kichern) as she touched George on the wing. "Feel how soft their feathers are," She touched George again, rubbing his head, neck and feet.

George laughed out loud, "HA! HA! HA! HA!" The woman and the man ran away.

"Why did you have to laugh, George?", Ann asked.

"She was tickling (kitzeln) me!", George said.

So nobody bought the ravens and they still live in the Tower of London, and England is still a mighty country.

True or false?

	True	False
The ravens never liked living at the Tower.	☐	☐
They liked watching people.	☐	☐
Every day tourists took 500 pictures of George.	☐	☐
The ravens were good at flying.	☐	☐
Without the ravens at the Tower England wouldnot be a mighty country.	☐	☐
The children did not buy the ravens because theydid not like them.	☐	☐
The woman did not touch George.	☐	☐
George laughed because the woman looked silly.	☐	☐

III WRITING TASK

Look at the pictures an write a story of about 120-150 words.

TEST 8

I FOCUS ON GRAMMAR

1. Find the correct modal verbs:

1. ______________________ (dürfen) I borrow your pen?
2. I have no time. I ____________________ (müssen) leave now. My parents are waiting for me.
3. I was tired last night but I ______________________ (nicht können) sleep.
4. I ______________________ (müssen) go to the bank yesterday to get some money.
5. This is a secret. You ______________________ (nicht dürfen) tell anybody.
6. It's late. I think we ______________________ (müssen) go home now.
7. Susan got the job because she ______________________ (können) speak five languages.
8. I can hear you clearly, you ______________________ (nicht müssen) shout.
9. The fire spread through the building quickly but everyone ________________ (können) escape (=entkommen).

2. Complete the following if-clauses:

1. If I were in San Francisco right now, I ____________________ (take) a picture of the famous Golden Gate Bridge.
2. Somebody will break into the house if you ______________________ (not lock) the door.
3. I would not believe the story of "The Missing Diamond Ring" if I _________________ (find) it in a newspaper.
4. Please call me if you ______________________ (decide) to go to the cinema in the evening.
5. If you _______________ (be) a vampire, you would not be able to see yourself in the mirror.
6. What would you do if somebody __________________ (try) to rob you?

3. Use the present perfect tense simple or progressive:

1. I ________________________________ (try) to solve the problem all afternoon, but I still ______________________________ (not find) out what's wrong.
2. We ______________________________ (watch) this stupid film since lunchtime. Let's switch over to another channel.
3. I'm sorry, I'm late. __________________________________ (you, wait) long ?
4. Bob and I went to school together. We __________________________ (be) friends ever since.
5. I remember meeting your sister last summer, but I ________________________ (not see) her this year.

II READING COMPREHENSION

Read the text, then do the tasks below:

Sophia Fowler Gallaudet was the deaf wife of Thomas Hopkins Gallaudet, who founded the first public school for the deaf in Hartford, Connecticut USA). She did not allow her deafness to prevent her from leading a normal life. She was educated, raised a family, ran a busy household, and helped to found Gallaudet College.

Sophia Fowler was born deaf near Guilford, Connecticut, on March 20, 1798. At that time, there were no schools for the deaf in America. However, Sophia was very clever. She learned many skills by watching the people around her. She learned to cook and sew, and became a charming young lady.

Sophia was nineteen years old when her parents learned that a school for the deaf had been founded in Hartford, Connecticut. She entered the school in 1817 and stayed there until the spring of 1821. While she was there, the principal of the school, Thomas Hopkins Gallaudet fell in love with her and asked her to marry him. Sophia married him in 1821.

As Mrs. Gallaudet, she continued to charm the people she met. She wanted to learn from every social situation. Through her contact with the many visitors to her home, she was actually able to continue her education.

Thomas Hopkins Gallaudet died in 1851, leaving his wife to make a life without him. However, her eight children did not leave her without support. With the help of her grown children, she continued to look after those children that had not yet left the house.

During her last years, Mrs. Gallaudet spent the winters in Washington, D.C., and the rest of the year travelling and visiting her children and grandchildren. She died on May 13, 1877.

deaf – taub   to prevent – hindern an   to found – gründen

a) Mark the correct answers:

1. Sophia Fowler Gallaudet was born
   a) in Hartford, Conneticut
   b) in Washington, D.C.
   c) near Guildford, Conneticut
   d) in New York

2. Sophia studied at the school for the deaf in Hartford, Connecticut
   a) for ten years
   b) from 1817 to 1851
   c) from 1817 to 1821
   d) from 1798 to 1803

3. The text tells us that Sophia
   a) tried to lead a normal life
   b) never went to school
   c) was not very clever
   d) never had children

4. After her husband died, Mrs Gallaudet finished raising her children, and then she:

a) moved to Washington, D.C.

b) spent her winters in Washington and the rest of the year visiting her children and grandchildren.

c) became sick.

d) never left the house again.

b) Mark the statements "true" (T) or "false" (F):

	True	False
Sophia Gallaudet was born on March 20, 1798.		
Mrs Gallaudet had seven children.		
Mrs Gallaudet became deaf when she was nineteen.		
Mrs Gallaudet's husband died in 1857.		
During her last years Mrs Gallaudet spent her winters in Washington, D.C,		

III WRITING TASK

Look at the pictures, then write a text of about 120-150 words.

TEST 9

I FOCUS ON GRAMMAR

1. Write down what they have been doing, complete the sentences using for or since

1. My sister ______________________ (talk) on the phone _________ 50 minutes.
2. My brother ______________________ (watch) TV _________ four in the afternoon.
3. My dad ______________________ (sleep) in front of the TV set _________ five.
4. My mum ______________________ (have) a shower _________ at least fifteen minutes.
5. I'm the only person in this household who ______________________ (do) any real work _________ days.

2. Complete the following if-clauses:

1. If vampires really existed we ______________________ (have to be) really careful .
2. Please call me if you ______________________ (need) any help.
3. Mrs Harris would be quite surprised if she ______________________ (know) that Detective Alex Caine suspected (=verdächtigen) her of murder.
4. I will not go to London in summer if I ______________________ (not get) a cheap flight.
5. Mr Connor ______________________ (love) to spend a week in Florida if he had more money.

3. Use the present perfect tense or the past tense (key words):

H: Hello John!

J: Hello Henry! Imagine! Yesterday I ______________________ (want) to buy a ticket to St.Ives.

H: St.Ives! Oh, I ______________________ (be, already) there twice. It's a lovely place.

J: Yes, I know, but I ______________________ (not go) there yesterday because I ____________________ (miss) the bus. The bus driver who told me that I had missed the bus was really arrogant. I tell you, I ______________________ (never, meet) such an arrogant person before. And how ______________________ (be) your holiday in New York?

H: I really ____________________ (enjoy) it. By the way, I ______________________ (send) you a postcard.

J: Oh, that's nice, thank you. But I ______________________ (not get) it yet.

II READING COMPREHENSION

Read the text, then mark the statements 'true' (T) or 'false' (F):

The Everglades

There are National Parks all over the Earth, but there is only one Everglades National Park, and it is in Florida. The Everglades is a most unusual and amazing habitat (=natürlicher Lebensraum). The Everglades is a 50-mile-wide, slow-moving river full of saw grass, which is why it is nick-named the River of Grass. The river of grass begins at Lake Okeechobee, a Native American word that means "Big Waters."

Lake Okeechobee is like no other lake on Earth. It covers 730 square miles and is an average of 15 feet deep. When the waters of Lake Okeechobee overflow, they flow into the River of Grass and move slowly toward the ocean.

There are two seasons in the Everglades: wet and dry. Conditions go from one extreme to another. Sometimes there is enough food and water, other times it is extremely difficult to find anything to eat.

Many animals live in the Everglades. In the wet season there is plenty to eat and drink. In the dry season, the living is not as easy. The waters dry up in some spots. Fresh water collects in ponds called solution holes. Animals live and hunt around these ponds to be near to something to drink. Perhaps the most famous resident (=Bewohner) in the Everglades is the alligator, which lives at the top of the food chain.

	True	False
The Everglades National Park is a wilderness area in California.		
The Native American word Okeechobee means "Big Water".		
Lake Okeechobee is an average of 20 feet deep.		
There are three season in the Everglades.		
In the wet season there is plenty of food and water.		
There is always enough water.		
The most famous animal in the Everglades is the alligator.		

III WRITING TASK

Look at the pictures, then write a text of about 120-150 words.

TEST 10

I FOCUS ON GRAMMAR

1. Complete the following if-sentences:

1. In India poor families believe that if a girl ______________________ (not get married) before she is fifteen, she will never get married.
2. Marion is thirteen and quite happy at the moment. But if she had a problem, she ______________________ (write) to an agony aunt.
3. If I was in Florida, I ______________________ (visit) Disney World and the Kennedy Space Center.

2. Adjective or adverb?

Suzanne moved ____________ (slow) along the river. She saw alligators with their ____________ (ugly) mouths full of ____________ (sharp) teeth. She noticed piranhas which were ____________ (dangerous) too. They swam very ____________ (fast) and could kill ____________ (quick). But the ____________ (small) insects were the worst. Then she saw a ____________ (poisonous) snake, which was ____________ (asleep). She walked ____________ (quiet) round a tree until she was ____________ (safe) again. Suzanne felt ____________ (weak) but she was not afraid. She was ____________ (lucky) because she knew the rules of the jungle ____________ (good).

3. Fill in the correct forms of the verbs "can, may, must". Be careful with the tenses!

1. Joanna ______________________ (cannot) make the lemon cookies because she didn't have all the ingredients (Zutaten).
2. Bob ______________________ (must) go shoppping for his mother next Tuesday.
3. When her mother was ill Nancy ______________________ (must) do the cooking.
4. Next weekend the children ______________________ (may) invite as many children as they want.
5. The children ______________________ (need not) go shopping because there were still enough tins in the cupboard.

II READING COMPREHENSION

Read the text, then do the tasks below:

Part-time jobs for teenagers

Among American students part-time jobs are very popular. Besides working in fast food restaurants and small cafeterias, baby sitting is a very popular job for a teenager in

America. Baby sitting is very popular among teenage girls and a good baby sitter can earn quite a bit if she is reliable (=verlässlich), responsible and mature (=reif). It is not necessarily an easy job.
A good baby sitter should know how to change diapers (=Windeln) and earn the respect of the children she is watching. She must be able to get the children ready for bed and keep an eye on them even while they are sleeping. In addition, she should be able to handle any unexpected emergency (=Notfall) and be calm at all times. She should know the emergency numbers of the hospital and police for difficult situations.
Once the children are asleep the baby sitter is free to watch TV or listen to music.
As a baby sitter you often have to work on Friday and Saturday nights when many married couples like to spend the night going to a movie or the theater.
Other part-time jobs which are popular especially among young boys are managing a paper route or mowing the lawns of people in one's neighborhood. These jobs can be a source of good income (=gute Einnahmequelle) for a high school student. Young boys who run paper routes have to get up early in the morning. This job has no holidays and the newspaper has to be delivered every day without exception. In America there are no newspaper holidays.
During the winter a snowstorm can become another source of income for a teenager.
The young boys make their rounds through their neighborhood equipped with a shovel and offer to clear driveways or to dig out a car buried in a meter of snow.
With these jobs the young people learn how to become part of the adult world.

A) Choose the correct answer:

1. Which is a very popular part time job for American girl students?
   - a) working for a newspaper
   - b) shop assistant
   - c) baby sitting
   - d) cleaning a neighbour's house

2. Which is a popular job for young boys?
   - a) baby sitting
   - b) a paper route
   - c) shop assistant
   - d) gas station attendant

3. A part time job gives young people a chance to earn money but it also
   - a) helps them to make new friends
   - b) fills up free time
   - c) teaches them responsibility
   - d) keeps them off the street

4. What is the disadvantage (=Nachteil) of a morning paper route?

a) There are no holidays
b) It often rains in the morning.
c) Students are often late for school.
d) The students get little money.

5. Why do young boys enjoy a winter snowstorm?

a) There is no school when it snows.
b) They can make snowmen and igloos.
c) They can go skiing and snowboarding.
d) They can make money shoveling snow.

6. How many newspaper holidays are there in America?

a) There are four, one in each saeson.
b) There are two, one in spring and one in autumn/fall.
c) There are none.
d) There are 12, one in every month.

B) Finish the following sentences:

1. Baby sitting is very popular.....
2. As a baby sitter you often have to.....
3. A baby sitter must get the children....
4. When the children are asleep the baby sitter....
5. A boy with a paper route has to.....
6. As a paper boy you ....

III WRITING TASK

Ghosts have always fascinated you. About a week ago you came back from a trip to a haunted castle (=Spukschloss).

Write a letter to a Ghost Club.
Tell them what you heard and saw during your stay at the haunted castle. (±120-150 words)
Use sentence starters (first – then; suddenly; later; finally; after a while . . .)
and make paragraphs!
Use at least 5 of the following words and phrases somewhere in your letter:

to go on a tour of a castle / tour guide (= Fremdenführerin) / to explain (= erklären) / portrait gallery / Duke of Blueberry Castle / murdered / to haunt (spuken) / to appear / strange / frightened / mysterious / to ask for help /to faint (=ohnmächtig werden)

Test 11

I FOCUS ON GRAMMAR

1. Fill in the correct form of the past perfect tense:

1. I hardly recognised her younger brother. He ______________________________ (change) a lot.
2. My aunt no longer had her car. She ___________________________ (sell) it.
3. Paula played squash yesterday. She wasn't very good at it because she ______________________________ (never, play) squash in her life.
4. Andrew was a complete stranger to me. I _________________________ (never, meet) him before.
5. Margaret was late for work. Her boss was very surprised. She __________________________ (never, be) late before.
6. My sister wasn't at home when I arrived. She _______________________________ (just, go) out.

2. Use reported speech

1. Mr Brown told us, "I was on my way home when I saw a strange thing crossing the road in front of my car. I stopped and got out. The thing looked like a dinosaur. I am sure I saw Nessie. I think I will write a book about Nessie."
2. Mrs Grant told the police, "My son went into the mountains alone yesterday. He is looking for minerals there. He often does that. He has just called me on the phone. I think he has lost his way. You must find him. I am afraid something terrible will happen to him."
3. Sue's American penfriend Claudia wrote, "We went camping in the mountains last weekend. Unfortunately it rained on Saturday and it was very slippery. My brother fell and lost his backpack. It took us two hours to find it again."
4. He promised, "I will never leave you again."

II READING COMPREHENSION

Nessie of Loch Ness

Loch Ness is the home of perhaps the most famous mystery of our time.

Loch Ness, the largest freshwater lake in the British Isles, is twenty-four miles long and, at one point, one and a half miles wide. It is about four hundred and fifty feet deep and at some places much deeper. It is cold and dark. In short, it is the perfect place to hide a monster.

Many lakes in Northern Scotland have ancient legends about monsters that were never written down. One story tells of Saint Columba who saved a swimmer from a hungry monster in the Ness river near Loch Ness in 565 A.D. This story was written down in the book *The Life of Saint Columba* in the late 7th Century.

In 1933 after a new road was built along the edge (Rand) of the Loch, more and more people said that they had seen the monster. On April 14 the owners of an inn (Gasthaus) in Drumnadrochit, the Mackays, watched an enormous animal swimming in the Loch. They told

Alex Campbel about it. Campbel spent a lot of time at the lake and saw the monster himself several times after the Mackays had told him about it.

Campbel described the creature as having "a long neck, about 6 feet long, and a smallish head that looked like a snake's head, and a huge hump (Buckel) behind..." Campbel thought the "monster" was about thirty feet long.

The first photograph of the thing was taken in 1933 by Hugh Gray. Gray reported, "I immediately got my camera ready and snapped the object which was then two to three feet above (oberhalb) the surface (Oberfläche) of the water. I did not see any head, because this was under the water, but I saw the tail (Schwanz) moving."

Maybe the most famous picture of the Loch Ness monster was the photo taken by Colonel Robert Wilson in 1934. It shows a long, thin neck rising above the water connected to a hump-like body. Today people think that this photo is a fake (Fälschung), because Christian Spurling admitted (zugeben) that he had helped build the model monster that was photographed. He admitted this shortly before he died in 1993 at age 90.

Early in 1934 Arthur Grant, a young veterinary student, was out on his motorcycle one evening when he almost ran into the monster as it crossed the road. Grant said the thing looked like a plesiosaurus. The plesiosaurus, a contemporary (Zeitgenosse) of the dinosaurs, was thought to have been extinct (ausgestorben) for at least 65 million years.

In April of 1960, Tim Dinsdale, while visiting the lake, made the first film of the monster. Although many scientists thought that the monster in his fim was really a motorboat. Dinsdale gave up his career as an engineer and spent the next twenty years of his life looking for the monster. Today we still do not know if the monster really exists.

True or false?

	true	false
Loch Ness is the largest lake in the world.	☐	☐
Saint Columba saved a swimmer in Loch Ness.	☐	☐
In 1933 many people said they saw the monster.	☐	☐
The monster's neck was thirty feet long.	☐	☐
The most famous photo was taken in 1933.	☐	☐
Christian Spurling helped build a model monster.	☐	☐
Arthur Grant saw the monster outside the Loch.	☐	☐
The first film of the monster was made in 1934.	☐	☐
Dinsdale looked for the monster for 20 years.	☐	☐

III WRITING TASK

Write a story using the following words:

Summer day – John – bike – huge animal – dinosaur – dangerous – to believe – to laugh – journalist – scientists – to watch – famous

Test 12

I FOCUS ON GRAMMAR

1. Make passive sentences:

1. the museum / build / 60 years ago (past tense)
2. the kids / send home / their teacher (future tense)
3. the thief / arrest / the police (future tense)
4. a lot of tickets / sell (present perfect tense)
5. the cake / make / the day before (past perfect tense)
6. German / speak / in Switzerland too (present tense)

2. Fill in the correct tense (present simple/continuous, past simple/continuous, past perfect, present perfect simple/continuous, future)

1. Last year I ____________________ (spend) my holidays in England. I ________________ ________________ (be) there before. But last year ________________ (be) different because I ____________________ (stay) with my friends. When I ____________________ (arrive) at the airport my friends ______________________________________ (wait) for me.
2. ____________________ (you/ever/see) such a good film?
   Well, I ____________________ (not be) to the cinema for some time now,
   but I ____________________ (see) Lord of the Rings last year and
   I ____________________ (like) it.
3. Tom, what ____________________ (you do)? Stop it! Leave the cat alone!
   You ____________________ (hurt) it! If you ____________________
   ____________________ (not stop), I ____________________ (call) mother.
4. Dogs are nice animals. They ____________________ (play) with their humans and ____________________ (sleep) a lot. Dogs ____________________ ____________________ (live) with humans for thousands of years.

II READING COMPREHENSION

William Shakespeare

Although William Shakespeare is maybe the most famous English writer of all times, we know very little about his life.

William Shakespeare was born in Stratford-upon-Avon on April 23, 1564. His father, John Shakespeare, was a glove maker and merchant (Händler). William had seven siblings three of whom died when they were still children.

Maybe William attended (besuchte) the grammar school in Stratford. People think so because the writer knew Latin (Latein) and Classical Greek (Altgriechisch).

In 1582 William Shakespeare married Anne Hathaway, who was eight years older than William.

Their first daughter was called Susanna. Later the Shakespeares had twins, Hamnet and Judith. Hamnet died at the age of 11.

The next thing we know about Shakespeare is that he moved to London where he became an actor and began to write plays for the theatre. Shakespeare's theatre company became the most successful in London. In Shakespeare's times all the roles were played by men or boys.

In those days the Globe Theatre was built on the south bank (Ufer) of the river Thames. There many of Shakespeare's plays were performed.

William Shakespeare wrote many plays, which are still performed in theatres all over the world today. He wrote comedies like "As You Like It" or "A Midsummer Night's Dream" and tragedies like "King Lear" or "Hamlet". His most popular tragedy is probably "Romeo and Juliet", which tells the sad story of two young lovers who cannot come together because their families hate each other.

Shakespeare's plays were very popular in his days and they still are today. Some people think that nobody has ever written better about human feelings and emotions than he did.

Shakespeare died in 1616. The legend says that he died on his birthday but this is probably not true.

True or false

	True	False
A lot is known about Shakespeare's life.	☐	☐
John Shakespeare had eight children.	☐	☐
Shakespeare's wife was younger than William.	☐	☐
In Shakespeare's days there were no actresses.	☐	☐
The Globe Theatre was built by Shakespeare.	☐	☐
Many theatres still perform Shakespeare's plays.	☐	☐
"King Lear" is one of Shakespeare's comedies.	☐	☐
We are sure that Shakespeare died on his birthday.	☐	☐
"As You Like It" is Shakespeare's most popular play.	☐	☐

II WRITING TASK

Look at the pictures and write a story of about 120-150 words.

Test 13

I English in Use

1. Past or Past Perfect?

1. Irene ______________________ (be) afraid of dogs because when she was a child a big dog ______________________ (bite) her.
2. Last week something really strange ______________________ (happen). My brother and I ________________ (ride) our bikes to the old cave in the wood. After three hours of exploring (erforschen) the cave we ______________ (be) really exhausted. We ________________ (want) to go back home but we ______________________ (forget) to lock our bikes and now they ______________________ (be) gone.
3. Sally was shocked when she __________________ (notice) that he husband ______________ (forget) to lock the house. Thank God nobody ______________________ (break) in!

2. Make passive sentences:

1. all the questions / must answer / the students (present tense)
2. the book /write / a famous author (past tense)
3. the letter / type / on the computer (past perfect tense)
4. some interesting questions / discuss / at the meeting (future tense)
5. my friends / inform / e-mail (present perfect tense)

3. Link the sentences using relative pronouns:

1. This is my aunt Sally. She knows a lot of interesting stories.
2. Can I talk to Mr. Brown? He knows everything about my problem.
3. Yesterday I found the book. I had bought it last month.
4. Tim lives across the street. He is a clever boy.
5. Can you see the flower? It is hidden behind the bush.

II READING COMPREHENSION

The rainforest

Around the Equator there is a broad band of rain forests. Nowhere else is there such a rich mixture of life, nowhere else are there so many secrets we still have to discover. There are plants that might help us to cure (heilen) dangerous illnesses and lots of interesting and rare animals.

Although the rainforests have so much to offer, they are "eaten up" alarmingly fast. Whether it is Central and South America, Africa or countries in the Far East like Malaysia or the Philippines, the story is the same. Rainforests are being destroyed so that man can have fields and sell the wood of the rainforest trees. About half the world's rainforest has already disappeared. An area the size of England, Scotland and Wales is burnt down every year.

Because of the destruction (Zerstörung) of the rainforests many species are killed.
About 50 a day, or one every half hour, disappear off the face of the earth.
There are about 200 million people living in the rainforests. They know how to survive in the forest, which plants to eat, which plants are medicines. But their lands are in danger.
Many plants that grow in the rainforests can be used in medicine. The rosy periwinkle (Immergrün) helps children to survive the blood disease leukaemia. Beautiful orchids are exported but they really belong in the tropics.
There are thick layers (Schichten) of vegetation between the forest floor and the treetops.
Most creatures live just below the treetops. Some exotic animals only live in the rainforest.
Some are very rare (selten) like the lemurs of Madagascar or the mountain gorillas of Rwanda.

Choose the answer which tells what the text really says:

1. The tropical rainforests of the world are
   a) an area the size of England, Scotland and Wales
   b) being "eaten up" very quickly
   c) in the Far East

2. Rainforest people
   a) probably live in the rainforest
   b) are dangerous
   c) are about 200 million in number

3. The rosy periwinkle
   a) belongs in the tropics
   b) has helped cure a children's blood disease
   c) is very expensive

4. Most rainforest creatures live
   a) just below the treetops
   b) on the forest floor
   c) in thick layers of vegetation between the forest floor and the treetops

III WRITING TASK

Continue the following story:

Linda, Paul and their parents were spending their holiday on Sicily. On a bright sunny day they made a trip to mount Etna, a famous volcano. They were walking up the mountain when Linda saw smoke coming out of the mountain. Suddenly ....

The following words may be useful:

to erupt – (ausbrechen (Vulkan)
lava – (Lava)
ashes – (Asche)

Aufsteigen in ...

Berger, Astrid; Broniowski, Gabriele
Aufsteigen in Englisch 3
So schaffst du die 3. Klasse HS/AHS/NMS
(mit Lösungsheft)

Kt., 80 Seiten, Format 21 x 29,7 cm
978-3-7074-0525-5-5

Berger, Astrid; Broniowski, Gabriele
Aufsteigen in Englisch 4
So schaffst du die 4. Klasse HS/AHS/NMS
(mit Lösungsheft)

Kt., 80 Seiten, Format 21 x 29,7 cm
978-3-7074-0761-7

www.ggverlag.at

1. Auflage 2008, Nachdruck 2012 (1,03)

Illustrationen: Paul Mangold und Elena Obermüller
Umschlaggestaltung: Pia Moest
Gesamtherstellung: Imprint, Ljubljana

ISBN 978-3-7074-1072-3

Aufsteigen ... Englisch 3 Schularbeiten

LÖSUNGSHEFT

G&G

TEST 1

I FOCUS ON GRAMMAR

1

1. Some years ago Liam **flew** to Valemount, Canada, to visit his father. One day he **went** fishing with his friend Ulva. When they **saw** some dark clouds, they **tried** to build a shelter. On the way back Liam **hurt** his leg but a search party **found** them.
2. **Have you ever had** such an exciting adventure? - No, but I think a trip to Canada would be fun.
3. "Would you like to go cycling with me?" Sam asked. "Sorry, I can't" Tom answered."
   I **have not finished /haven't finished** studying for the test."
4. Do you know Mike, our neighbour's son? -Yes, I do.-Well, he **dyed** his hair green yesterday.- That's cool. I **have never dyed** my hair before, because my mother thinks I'll look awful.

2

Last year my parents and I stayed at a little campsite in Yosemite Park. **First** we put up our tent and then we wanted to roast some marshmallows. My dad told me to get some firewood, so we could make a fire.
Finally we were sitting in front of our tent enjoying our marshmallows. **From time** to time we heard strange noises. I was afraid but my dad said that these noises were nothing unusual in the wilderness. **Suddenly** we saw two racoons coming towards us. We quickly ran to our car and got inside.
The racoons ate all our food. **After several minutes** the racoons left again.

3

1. It took Mrs Kerny three hours to do the ironing.
2. It took her twenty minutes to load the dishwasher.
3. It took the rescue team two days to find the survivors of the plane crash.

4

1. When I phoned my friends they **were playing** a new computer game.
2. When Bob **was doing** the washing up he cut his finger.
3. I **was walking** to school when a dog attacked me.
4. My sister **was watching** her favourite TV series when the telephone rang.
5. Yesterday at seven I **was preparing** dinner for my family.

II READING COMPREHENSION

	True	False
Winter is the hunting season, so they went hunting in January.	x	
The Range Rover had four-wheel-drive.	x	
During the first two hours they found animals to hunt.		x
The falcon could not catch the rabbit.		x
The group sat around the fire until late in the evening.	x	
They could not go on because they ran out of petrol.		x
Karim walked for more than four hours.	x	
Karim did not know the way and got lost.		x
Karim met a man on a camel.	x	
The man took Karim to a road.	x	

TEST 2

I FOCUS ON GRAMMAR

1

1. If you train your dog, it **will guard your house**.
2. He will buy a guinea pig for his children if they **promise** to take care of it.
3. If she goes on holiday, her brother **usually looks after** her pets.
4. I will take riding lessons if I **am not allergic** to horses.

2

1. Tom is as tall as John. Peter is taller than John and Tom. John /Tom is shorter than Peter.
   Oder: Tom and John are shorter than Peter.
2. There are fewer people at the cinema than at the theatre/the concert/the theatre and the concert.
   There are more people at the theatre/the concert than at the cinema.
3. The jeans are as expensive as the shoes. The T-shirt is cheaper than the jeans/the shoes/the jeans and the shoes.

3

1. They **were playing** Monopoly when they heard a terrible cry.
2. I **was doing** my homework when the computer broke down.
3. The girl in the thriller **was waiting** for her father when she **saw** a strange man with a woman and a little boy.
4. When the Inspector **knocked** at the door the suspects **were watching** TV.

4

1. We **have not/haven't seen** Charles since May. I don't know what he is doing.
2. The rain has stopped. The sun **is shining** now. Let's go out!
3. She **will/is going** to pick up her aunt at the station tomorrow.
4. **Have you ever read** any of the "Harry Potter" books?
5. Yesterday Kate and Susan **showed** me the photos they **took/had taken** in London in summer.
6. You **need not/don't have to** do the homework today.

TEST 3

I FOCUS ON GRAMMAR

1

1. They chatted **happily** all afternoon because they had not seen each other since the holidays.
2. Susan is a very good student. She always does her homework **carefully**.
3. My brother always looks **angry** after talking to my dad. He thinks our dad is too strict.
4. Jennifer felt **terribly** cold when she came home from a walk with the dog.
5. Paul didn't want to miss the bus, so he ran very **fast** to catch it.
6. They got stuck in a traffic jam so they **nearly** missed the plane.
7. Are you sure you want to eat this soup? It tastes **awful**.

2

1. **Have you ever tried** bungee jumping? - Yes, I did that last year, but I think it's too dangerous.

2. I hope Aunt Jane **will come** to visit us next week. I haven't seen her for weeks.
3. In 2002 Fred **did not understand** a word of English, but now he speaks it quite well.
4. Right now my mother **is buying** food at the supermarket. She **goes** there every Thursday.
5. Do you know what **happened** yesterday? I **was watching** my favourite TV show when we suddenly **had** a power failure (=Stromausfall).

3

1. Maria will get you some money if she **goes** to the bank.
2. You have a bad cold. If you go to the doctor he **will tell** you what to do.
3. If he hits his little brother, his father always **punishes** him.
4. If my alarm clock does not go off I **am always** late for school.
5. I'll give her a call if I **find** her phone number. I don't know where I put it.

II READING COMPREHENSION

Deine Sätze könnten so ausschauen:

1. In the morning Kim runs out into the garden and starts gnawing on a piece of wood.
2. To get to the inside of soft toy Kim uses her teeth and claws.
3. Her human thinks that she is the boss.
4. In the woods Kim thinks it is fun to run around without a leash, to sniff at the trees and to jump into the river.
5. Kim loves playing but she also likes eating and sleeping.

TEST 4

I FOCUS ON GRAMMAR

1

1. Last night I **was reading** in bed when I suddenly heard a scream.
2. **Were you watching** television last night when I phoned you?
3. I **broke** a plate last night. I **was doing** the washing up when it **slipped** out of my hand.
4. Someone **ran** off with my clothes while I **was swimming**.
5. The thieves **were breaking** in while we **were sleeping**.

2

1. We **have not been** to the cinema since June.
2. It **is raining** now. Let's not go out!
3. We **will be able to meet** him at the airport tomorrow.
4. **Have you ever watched** "Spongebob"?
5. Yesterday Tina **showed** me the video she had made at Christmas.
6. Last year I **walked** to the office every day.

3

1. We have lots of time, we **need not** hurry.
2. Last year he **had to** give up smoking.
3. They think he **will be able** to leave the hospital in 4 days.
4. Sorry, I didn't come yesterday but I **was not allowed** to leave my room.
5. I **must not** forget to phone George.
6. Why **did you have** to leave so early yesterday?
7. This is a wonderful book! You **must** read it!
8. I didn't like the soup at all. I was very happy I **did not have to** eat it.

9. I'm very busy tomorrow. So I **won't be able** to see you.
10. **Can** you open the window, please? It's hot in here!
11. Oh, you **need not** help me. I can do it myself.
12. Be careful! We **must not** break the window!

II READING COMPREHENSION

We can be sure that ghosts exist.	false
John Harris built Eldon House.	false
Sarah's boy-friend was a young officer.	true
Wynniatt did not want to come to the party.	false
Sarah saw Wynniatt at the party.	true
Wynniatt's body was found in the river Thames.	false
The ghost of an old man appears in Eldon House.	false

TEST 5

I FOCUS ON GRAMMAR

1

1. Imagine, Tim missed his flight, so he **had to** spend a night in an expensive hotel and **could** only fly the next day.
2. **Were you allowed** to go to the cinema yesterday?
3. Sorry, I **won't be able** to go to the match with you next Monday.
4. You **don't have to/need not** wait for me.
5. I know that Patrick **was not allowed** to go to the concert last week because of his bad marks.
6. We **will have to walk /must walk** to school if my mother doesn't take us there by car.
7. In the evening we **must not** be too loud because of our neighbour's baby.
8. Imagine, we **did not have to** pay for the tickets last night, they gave them to us for free.

2

1. Yesterday was a perfect day as there were no clouds **in** the sky.
2. Who is that old lady **in** the picture? She looks familiar.
3. Mrs. Anderson's office is **on** the second floor.
4. We always get a lot of homework **on** Friday.
5. Her father thinks that **at** 13 Mary is too young to go to the disco.
6. I left all my English books **at** school because we have no homework today.
7. She has been **on** the phone for hours! Who is she talking to?
8. Where is your dad? –He is **at** work.
9. Could you put he book **on** the table, please?
10. She wants to live **in** the country because the air is much cleaner there.
11. **In** July they always go on holiday with their parents.

3

I'm sure **someone/somebody** will be there to help you with the suitcase.
I can't see my mother **anywhere**. Do you know where she is?
We can't see **anything**. It's so dark in here.
Some people are really terrible. They can't remember **anything**.
The new bookshop is no good. There are not **any** interesting books.
Agnes was so shocked that she didn't say **anything**.

II READING COMPREHENSION

Choose the answer which tells what the text really says:

1. c
2. a
3. b

Deine Antworten könnten so aussehen.:

1. More whales were killed because the hunters had better harpoons, faster boats and better machines.
2. People hunt whales because they make money by selling the oil and the meat.

TEST 6

I FOCUS ON GRAMMAR

1

1. Last Saturday Tom met his friends at the cinema.
2. I have never eaten such a good pizza.
3. Sarah told me that she had found her keys.
4. They often meet at the park after school.
5. We have just finished our lunch.
6. Will you be at home in the evening?

2

On Tuesday Bill met his friends **in** the evening. They went **to** the cinema. The film began **at** 9 o'clock pm. Bill was sitting **behind** a very tall lady. **After** the film the friends went home by bus. **On** the next day Bill was very tired. **At** school he could not concentrate.

3

Yesterday I **was reading** a book when the phone **rang**. It **was** my friend Sandra. She **was waiting** for her train to arrive and **wanted** to know if I **had** time to meet her.
She **asked** me what I **was doing** at the moment. I **told** her I **was** free and that we could meet in 40 minutes. While I **was looking** for my keys my dog Wayne **was barking** all the time because he **wanted** to come with me.

II READING COMPREHENSION

Molly and the vampire next door

1. They did not see him because he was only active at night.
2. Cornelius lived in a tiny flat./He lived in the house next to Molly's house.
3. She was sad because she did not want to leave everything she loved./ She was sad because she did not want to move to a retirement home.
4. He died when Charles was 10 years old.
5. Archibald was Cornelius' cousin.
6. Archibald lived in Scotland/in a castle/in a castle in Scotland.
7. Hier muss deine eigene Antwort stehen.

TEST 7

I FOCUS ON GRAMMAR

1

Yesterday I **did not have to** help my mother with the washing up. It was my birthday and so my mother said I **was allowed to** read while my brother and my sister had to load the dishwasher and to clean the table.
In the evening I **could not** find my English book, so I **had to** call my friend who lives next door. She came and we did our homework together.
I am happy that I **do not have to** tell my English teacher today that I **could not/was not able to** do my homework yesterday.

2

While Sue was on holiday in Florida she stayed at her friend Barbara's house. **At** one of Barbara's parties she met this cool guy, Frank.
On the next day he called her in the morning.
"Do you want to meet me **on** Friday **at** seven o'clock?", he asked. Sue was so happy.
When Sue was **at** home again she told her friends about the great time she had had in Florida.
Before she went back to school she wrote a letter to Barbara to thank her for the wonderful holiday.

3

1. Can you hear that noise? I think our neighbour **is playing** the trumpet.
2. America **was discovered** in 1492.
3. Tigers **eat** meat.
4. Yesterday I **saw** my teacher at the cinema. When I **came** in she **Was talking** to a strange looking man.
5. Next year Paul **is going** to spend his holidays in Turkey.

II READING COMPREHENSION

The Ravens

The ravens never liked living at the Tower	false
They liked watching people	true
Every day tourists took 500 pictures of George	false
The ravens were good at flying	false
Without the ravens at the Tower England would not be a mighty country	true
The children did not buy the ravens because they did not like them	false
The woman did not touch George	false
George laughed because the woman looked silly	false

TEST 8

I FOCUS ON GRAMMAR

1

1. **May** I borrow your pen?
2. I have no time. I **must / have to** leave now. My parents are waiting for me.
3. I was tired last night but I **could not / was not able to** sleep.

4. I **had to** go to the bank yesterday to get some money.
5. This is a secret. You **must not** tell anybody.
6. It's late. I think we **must go** home now.
7. Susan got the job because she **can** speak five languages.
8. I can hear you clearly, you **need not / don not have to** shout.
9. The fire spread through the building quickly but everyone **could / was able to** escape (=entkommen).

2

1. If I were in San Francisco right now, I **would take** a picture of the famous Golden Gate Bridge.
2. Somebody will break into the house if you **do not lock** the door.
3. I would not believe the story of "The Missing Diamond Ring" if I **found** it in a newspaper.
4. Please call me if you **decide** to go to the cinema in the evening.
5. If you **were** a vampire, you would not be able to see yourself in the mirror.
6. What would you do if somebody **tried** to rob you?

3

1. I **have been trying** to solve the problem all afternoon, but I still **have not found** out what's wrong.
2. We **have been watching** this stupid film since lunchtime. Let's switch over to another channel.
3. I'm sorry, I'm late. **Have you been waiting** long?
4. Bob and I went to school together. We **have been** friends ever since.
5. I remember meeting your sister last summer, but I **have not seen** her this year.

II READING COMPREHENSION

A

1C / 2C / 3A / 4B

B

	True	False
Sophia Gallaudet was born on March 20, 1798.	x	
Mrs Gallaudet had seven children.		x
Mrs Gallaudet became deaf when she was nienteen.		x
Mrs Gallaudet's husband died in 1857.		x
During her last years Mrs Gallaudet spent her winters in Washington,D.C,	x	

TEST 9

I FOCUS ON GRAMMAR

1

1. My sister **has been talking** on the phone **for** 50 minutes.
2. My brother **has been watching** TV **since** four in the afternoon.
3. My dad **has been sleeping** in front of the TV set **since** five.
4. My mum **has been having** a shower **for** at least fifteen minutes.
5. I'm the only person in this household who **has been doing** any real work **for** days.

2

1. If vampires really existed we **would have to be** really careful.
2. Please call me if you **need** any help.
3. Mrs Harris would be quite surprised if she **knew** that Detective Alex Caine suspected (=verdächtigen) her of murder.
4. I will not go to London in summer if I **do not get** a cheap flight.
5. Mr Connor **would love** to spend a week in Florida if he had more money.

3

H: Hello John!
J: Hello Henry! Imagine! Yesterday, I **wanted** to buy a ticket to St. Ives.
H: St.Ives! Oh, I **have already been** there twice. It's a lovely place.
J: Yes, I know, but I **did not go** there yesterday because I **missed** the bus. The bus driver who told me that I had missed the bus was really arrogant. I tell you, I **have never met** such an arrogant person before. And how ________________ (be) your holiday in New York?
H: I really **enjoyed** it. By the way, I **sent** you a postcard.
J: Oh, that's nice, thank you. But I **have not got** it yet.

II READING COMPREHENSION

	True	False
The Everglades National Park is a wilderness area in California.	x	
The Native American word Okeechobee means "Big Water".	x	
Lake Okeechobee is an average of 20 feet deep.		x
There are three season in the Everglades.		x
In the wet season there is plenty of food and water.	x	
There is always enough water.		x
The most famous animal in the Everglades is the alligator.	x	

TEST 10

I FOCUS ON GRAMMAR

1

1. In India poor families believe that if a girl **does not get married** before she is fifteen, she will never get married.
2. Marion is thirteen and quite happy at the moment. But if she had a problem, she **would write** to an agony aunt.
3. If I was in Florida, I **would visit** Disney World and the Kennedy Space Center.

2

Sharon moved **slowly** along the river. She saw alligators with their **ugly** mouths full of **sharp** teeth. She noticed piranhas which were **dangerous** too. They swam very **fast** and could kill **quickly**. But the **small** insects were the worst. Then she saw a **poisonous** snake, which was asleep. She walked **quietly** round a tree until she was safe again. Sharon felt **weak** but she was not afraid. She was **lucky** because she knew the rules of the jungle well.

3

1. Joanna **could not / was not able to** make the lemon cookies because she didn't have all the ingredients (Zutaten).
2. Bob **will have to** go shoppping for his mother next Tuesday.
3. When her mother was ill Nancy **had to** do the cooking.
4. Next weekend the children **will be allowed to** invite as many children as they want.
5. The children **did not have to** go shopping because there were still enough tins in the cupboard.

II READING COMPREHENSION

A

1C / 2B / 3C / 4C / 5D / 6C

B

Deine Antworten könnten so aussehen:

1. Baby sitting is very popular among American teenage girls.
2. As a baby sitter you often have to work on Friday and Saturday nights.
3. A baby sitter must get the children ready for bed and keep an eye on them while they are sleeping.
4. When the children are asleep the baby sitter can watch TV or listen to music.
5. A boy with a paper route has to get up early every day.
6. As a paper boy you have no holidays.

TEST 11

I FOCUS ON GRAMMAR

1

1. I hardly recognised her younger brother. He **had changed** a lot.
2. My aunt no longer had her car. She **had sold** it.
3. Paula played squash yesterday. She wasn't very good at it because she had never played squash in her life.
4. Andrew was a complete stranger to me. I **had never met** him before.
5. Margaret was late for work. Her boss was very surprised. She **had never been** late before.
6. My sister wasn't at home when I arrived. She **had just gone** out.

2

1. Mr Brown told us that he **had been** on his way home when he **had seen** a strange thing crossing the road in front of his car. He **had stopped** and had got out. The thing **had looked** like a dinosaur. He **was** sure he **had seen** Nessie. He **thought** he **would write** a book about Nessie.
2. Mrs Grant told the police that her son **had gone** into the mountains alone **the day before.** She said that he **was** looking for minerals there. He often **did** that. He **had** just **called** her on the phone. She thought he had lost his way. They **had to find** him. She **was** afraid something terrible **would happen** to him."
3. Sue's American penfriend Claudia wrote **that they had gone** camping in the mountains **the weekend before**. Unfortunately it **had rained** on Saturday and it **had been** very slippery. Her brother **had fallen** and lost his backpack. It **had taken** them two hours to find it again."
4. He promised that he **would never leave** her again."

II READING COMPREHENSION

Nessie of Loch Ness

Loch Ness is the largest lake in the world	false
Saint Columba saved a swimmer in Loch Ness	false
In 1933 many people said they saw the monster	true
The monster's neck was thirty feet long	false
The most famous photo was taken in 1934	true
Christian Spurling helped build a model monster	true
Arthur Grant saw the monster outside the Loch	true
The first film of the monster was made in 1934	false
Dinsdale looked for the monster for 20 years	true

TEST 12

I FOCUS ON GRAMMAR

1

1. The museum was built 60 years ago.
2. The kids will be sent home by their teacher.
3. The thief will be arrested by the police.
4. A lot of tickets have been sold.
5. The cake had been made the day before
6. German is spoken in Switzerland too.

2

1. Last year I **spent** my holidays in England. I **had been** there before. But last year **was** different because I **was staying** with my friends. When I **arrived** at the airport my friends **were waiting** for me.
2. **Have you ever seen** such a good film? Well, I **have not been** to the cinema for some time now, but I **saw** Lord of the Rings last year and I **liked** it.
3. Tom, what **are you doing**? Stop it! Leave the cat alone! You **are hurting** it! If you **don't stop**, I will call mother.

Dogs are nice animals. They **play** with their humans and **sleep** a lot. Dogs **have been living** with humans for thousands of years.

II READING COMPREHENSION

William Shakespeare

A lot is known about Shakespeare's life	false
John Shakespeare had eight children	true
Shakespeare's wife was younger than William	false
In Shakespeare's days there were no actresses	true
The Globe Theatre was built by Shakespeare	false
Many theatres still perform Shakespeare's plays	true
"King Lear" is one of Shakespeare's comedies	false
We are sure that Shakespeare died on his birthday	false
"As You Like It" is Shakespeare's most popular play	false

TEST 13

I FOCUS ON GRAMMAR

1

1. Irene **was** afraid of dogs because when she was a child a big dog **had bitten** her.
2. Last week something really strange **happened**. My brother and I **rode** our bikes to the old cave in the wood. After three hours of exploring (=erforschen) the cave we **were** really exhausted. We **wanted** to go back home but we **had forgotten** to lock our bikes and now they **were** gone.
3. Sally was shocked when she **noticed** that her husband **had forgotten** to lock the house. Thank God nobody **had broken** in!

2

1. All the questions must be answered by the students.
2. The book was written by a famous author.
3. The letter had been typed on the computer.
4. Some interesting questions will be discussed at the meeting.
5. My friends have been informed by e-mail.

3

1. This is my aunt Sally **who** knows a lot of interesting stories.
2. Can I talk to Mr. Brown **who** knows everything about my problem?
3. Yesterday I found the book **which** I had bought last month.
4. Tim, **who** lives across the street, is a clever boy.
5. Can you see the flower **which** is hidden behind the bush?

II READING COMPREHENSION

1. b
2. c
3. b
4. a

Answer in complete sentences: Deine Antworten könnten so aussehen:

1. They are destroyed because people want to sell the wood of the trees and they are cut down to make room for fields.
2. The plants are important because they can be used as medicines.